Questions lovingly answered by:

_______________________ & _______________________

How do I love thee? Let me count the ways.
I love thee to the depth and breadth and height
My soul can reach, when feeling out of sight
For the ends of being and ideal grace.
I love thee to the level of every day's
Most quiet need, by sun and candle-light.
I love thee freely, as men strive for right.
I love thee purely, as they turn from praise.
I love thee with the passion put to use
In my old griefs, and with my childhood's faith.
I love thee with a love I seemed to lose
With my lost saints. I love thee with the breath,
Smiles, tears, of all my life; and, if God choose,
I shall but love thee better after death.

– Elizabeth Barrett Browning –

Do you ever have to deal with others? Why?

☐ HER REPLY ☐ HIS REPLY   ☐ HIS REPLY ☐ HER REPLY

What's something you have to tell everyone but you'll never tell anyone?

☐ HER REPLY ☐ HIS REPLY   ☐ HIS REPLY ☐ HER REPLY

What do you think it was?

☐ HER REPLY ☐ HIS REPLY   ☐ HIS REPLY ☐ HER REPLY

How would you describe the feeling of being stranded in another reality?

☐ HER REPLY ☐ HIS REPLY   ☐ HIS REPLY ☐ HER REPLY

If you had to choose one thing that you've learned about yourself over the past five years, what would it be?

☐ HER REPLY ☐ HIS REPLY

☐ HIS REPLY ☐ HER REPLY

Where's your favorite place to go?

☐ HER REPLY ☐ HIS REPLY

☐ HIS REPLY ☐ HER REPLY

When was the second time you said you really hated someone?

☐ HER REPLY ☐ HIS REPLY   ☐ HIS REPLY ☐ HER REPLY

What is one thing that you would like to make sure it's clear before you get started?

☐ HER REPLY ☐ HIS REPLY   ☐ HIS REPLY ☐ HER REPLY

What do your children need when they're feeling scared?

☐ HER REPLY ☐ HIS REPLY   ☐ HIS REPLY ☐ HER REPLY

Tell a memory you have with one of your uncles.

☐ HER REPLY ☐ HIS REPLY   ☐ HIS REPLY ☐ HER REPLY

Would you rather not be the hero or the villain?

☐ HER REPLY ☐ HIS REPLY

☐ HIS REPLY ☐ HER REPLY

What has made you feel the happiest during this year?

☐ HER REPLY ☐ HIS REPLY

☐ HIS REPLY ☐ HER REPLY

Why do you have this weird attitude?

☐ HER REPLY ☐ HIS REPLY

☐ HIS REPLY ☐ HER REPLY

What makes you feel most alive?

☐ HER REPLY ☐ HIS REPLY

☐ HIS REPLY ☐ HER REPLY

What have you done in your life that you are very proud of?

☐ HER REPLY ☐ HIS REPLY   ☐ HIS REPLY ☐ HER REPLY

How did you end up doing what you do?

☐ HER REPLY ☐ HIS REPLY   ☐ HIS REPLY ☐ HER REPLY

What is one thing that you're looking forward to as this year
goes on?

☐ HER REPLY ☐ HIS REPLY   ☐ HIS REPLY ☐ HER REPLY

Pretend you're a chef and tell me about your restaurant. What
foods do you serve?

☐ HER REPLY ☐ HIS REPLY   ☐ HIS REPLY ☐ HER REPLY

Do you feel sad or happy? Why or why not?

☐ HER REPLY ☐ HIS REPLY

☐ HIS REPLY ☐ HER REPLY

What's the best sound, smell, and taste you've had experienced?

☐ HER REPLY ☐ HIS REPLY

☐ HIS REPLY ☐ HER REPLY

Tell me about an award you have received.

☐ HER REPLY   ☐ HIS REPLY

☐ HIS REPLY   ☐ HER REPLY

Does your senses, thought, beliefs, feelings, and thoughts, change? How?

☐ HER REPLY   ☐ HIS REPLY

☐ HIS REPLY   ☐ HER REPLY

What's the single most important tip you have for staying sane while traveling alone in foreign lands?

☐ HER REPLY ☐ HIS REPLY   ☐ HIS REPLY ☐ HER REPLY

List of things that your foot would smash if you did it

☐ HER REPLY ☐ HIS REPLY   ☐ HIS REPLY ☐ HER REPLY

What's the weirdest smell you have ever smelled?

☐ HER REPLY ☐ HIS REPLY

☐ HIS REPLY ☐ HER REPLY

How would you describe the feeling of being declared bankrupt?

☐ HER REPLY ☐ HIS REPLY

☐ HIS REPLY ☐ HER REPLY

Which is more important to you, you're working and enjoying doing it or just going through your daily life? Why?

☐ HER REPLY ☐ HIS REPLY   ☐ HIS REPLY ☐ HER REPLY

Is there a time when you will be free of regret? Why?

☐ HER REPLY ☐ HIS REPLY   ☐ HIS REPLY ☐ HER REPLY

What is the most valuable thing to you?

☐ HER REPLY ☐ HIS REPLY   ☐ HIS REPLY ☐ HER REPLY

What is a great night like?

☐ HER REPLY ☐ HIS REPLY   ☐ HIS REPLY ☐ HER REPLY

How many books have you read?

☐ HER REPLY ☐ HIS REPLY

☐ HIS REPLY ☐ HER REPLY

What do you love most about your home?

☐ HER REPLY ☐ HIS REPLY

☐ HIS REPLY ☐ HER REPLY

If you had to choose the second best location in the world, why would you choose here?

□ HER REPLY □ HIS REPLY

□ HIS REPLY □ HER REPLY

How do you deal with people who hate you so much?

□ HER REPLY □ HIS REPLY

□ HIS REPLY □ HER REPLY

Has anyone ever influenced your manners for the better? Who?

☐ HER REPLY ☐ HIS REPLY   ☐ HIS REPLY ☐ HER REPLY

How would you describe the feeling of being alone in space and time?

☐ HER REPLY ☐ HIS REPLY   ☐ HIS REPLY ☐ HER REPLY

What was your favorite family dinner as a child?

☐ HER REPLY ☐ HIS REPLY

☐ HIS REPLY ☐ HER REPLY

What are you reading this morning?

☐ HER REPLY ☐ HIS REPLY

☐ HIS REPLY ☐ HER REPLY

What's the thing you most regret?

☐ HER REPLY ☐ HIS REPLY   ☐ HIS REPLY ☐ HER REPLY

What if you are given a second chance to be 18 again? What will you do? Will you change anything?

☐ HER REPLY ☐ HIS REPLY   ☐ HIS REPLY ☐ HER REPLY

What would you do if you saw someone completely in distress in the street?

☐ HER REPLY ☐ HIS REPLY

☐ HIS REPLY ☐ HER REPLY

Do you ever feel pressure to believe? Why?

☐ HER REPLY ☐ HIS REPLY

☐ HIS REPLY ☐ HER REPLY

Would you rather be able to command water or the wind? Why?

☐ HER REPLY ☐ HIS REPLY   ☐ HIS REPLY ☐ HER REPLY

Say something about the future

☐ HER REPLY ☐ HIS REPLY   ☐ HIS REPLY ☐ HER REPLY

When might it be bad to be honest?

☐ HER REPLY   ☐ HIS REPLY

☐ HIS REPLY   ☐ HER REPLY

How did you react when your child was upset?

☐ HER REPLY   ☐ HIS REPLY

☐ HIS REPLY   ☐ HER REPLY

Would you rather work with someone who gets paid to make games or one you'd rather learn from and get paid to make games?

☐ HER REPLY ☐ HIS REPLY   ☐ HIS REPLY ☐ HER REPLY

If you could run out to any restaurant right now with more than enough money, where would you go?

☐ HER REPLY ☐ HIS REPLY   ☐ HIS REPLY ☐ HER REPLY

How would you describe the feeling of being able to have your personal project or your work out in the world and see it in action?

☐ HER REPLY ☐ HIS REPLY   ☐ HIS REPLY ☐ HER REPLY

List of things that you would like to achieve in life

☐ HER REPLY ☐ HIS REPLY   ☐ HIS REPLY ☐ HER REPLY

If a friend asks you to keep a secret that you don't feel comfortable keeping, what would you do?

☐ HER REPLY ☐ HIS REPLY

☐ HIS REPLY ☐ HER REPLY

List of things that have solution for a day

☐ HER REPLY ☐ HIS REPLY

☐ HIS REPLY ☐ HER REPLY

What would you do if you had the ability to read minds for 24 hours?

☐ HER REPLY ☐ HIS REPLY   ☐ HIS REPLY ☐ HER REPLY

Will you still take on challenges that you aren't confident you can overcome? Why? Why not?

☐ HER REPLY ☐ HIS REPLY   ☐ HIS REPLY ☐ HER REPLY

What were the effects of the '90s?

☐ HER REPLY ☐ HIS REPLY   ☐ HIS REPLY ☐ HER REPLY

What's the last thing you did that you regret?

☐ HER REPLY ☐ HIS REPLY   ☐ HIS REPLY ☐ HER REPLY

Do you think a sixth sense exists? Explain.

☐ HER REPLY   ☐ HIS REPLY

☐ HIS REPLY   ☐ HER REPLY

When was the last time you broke someone's heart?

☐ HER REPLY   ☐ HIS REPLY

☐ HIS REPLY   ☐ HER REPLY

What would you have the other person say about you?

☐ HER REPLY ☐ HIS REPLY   ☐ HIS REPLY ☐ HER REPLY

What's your least favorite thing to do with your family?

☐ HER REPLY ☐ HIS REPLY   ☐ HIS REPLY ☐ HER REPLY

If you had to change your name, what would it be and what will be its meaning to you?

☐ HER REPLY ☐ HIS REPLY

☐ HIS REPLY ☐ HER REPLY

If you could tell one thing about the show that inspired you to go on the road, what would it be?

☐ HER REPLY ☐ HIS REPLY

☐ HIS REPLY ☐ HER REPLY

☐ HER REPLY ☐ HIS REPLY   ☐ HIS REPLY ☐ HER REPLY

☐ HER REPLY ☐ HIS REPLY   ☐ HIS REPLY ☐ HER REPLY

What is one thing you didn't learn today?

□ HER REPLY □ HIS REPLY

□ HIS REPLY □ HER REPLY

How would you describe the feeling of being bored?

□ HER REPLY □ HIS REPLY

□ HIS REPLY □ HER REPLY

Tell about a time you had a very troubling or enlightening dream.

☐ HER REPLY ☐ HIS REPLY   ☐ HIS REPLY ☐ HER REPLY

What might happen if you could actually make something so big and effective that people will want it?

☐ HER REPLY ☐ HIS REPLY   ☐ HIS REPLY ☐ HER REPLY

In what world would you want to go back in time and do something that could never happen to you?

☐ HER REPLY ☐ HIS REPLY   ☐ HIS REPLY ☐ HER REPLY

If you had to choose one thing to give to your dad as a token of appreciation for everything he gave you, what would it be?

☐ HER REPLY ☐ HIS REPLY   ☐ HIS REPLY ☐ HER REPLY

What's your personal journey that you would like to share?

☐ HER REPLY ☐ HIS REPLY

☐ HIS REPLY ☐ HER REPLY

Describe your favorite painting and what you think the artist was trying to create

☐ HER REPLY ☐ HIS REPLY

☐ HIS REPLY ☐ HER REPLY

What makes you feel the least comfortable?

☐ HER REPLY ☐ HIS REPLY

☐ HIS REPLY ☐ HER REPLY

How can you help your child deal with rejection?

☐ HER REPLY ☐ HIS REPLY

☐ HIS REPLY ☐ HER REPLY

What would you do if there were a universe of fate and every one of them had an infinite number of choices?

☐ HER REPLY ☐ HIS REPLY   ☐ HIS REPLY ☐ HER REPLY

How would you describe the feeling of being in love?

☐ HER REPLY ☐ HIS REPLY   ☐ HIS REPLY ☐ HER REPLY

If you could put your heart into every piece of a project, what would you consider the most memorable moment of it all?

☐ HER REPLY ☐ HIS REPLY   ☐ HIS REPLY ☐ HER REPLY

What do you do when you're a glass?

☐ HER REPLY ☐ HIS REPLY   ☐ HIS REPLY ☐ HER REPLY

What must you do to be productive at work?

☐ HER REPLY ☐ HIS REPLY   ☐ HIS REPLY ☐ HER REPLY

How would you describe the feeling of being heavier?

☐ HER REPLY ☐ HIS REPLY   ☐ HIS REPLY ☐ HER REPLY

What did you do today that made you laugh and feel happy?

☐ HER REPLY ☐ HIS REPLY

☐ HIS REPLY ☐ HER REPLY

How do you deal with people?

☐ HER REPLY ☐ HIS REPLY

☐ HIS REPLY ☐ HER REPLY

Would you rather eat ice cream or jelly?

☐ HER REPLY ☐ HIS REPLY   ☐ HIS REPLY ☐ HER REPLY

How do you encourage your children to feel safe in their skin?

☐ HER REPLY ☐ HIS REPLY   ☐ HIS REPLY ☐ HER REPLY

Would you choose a master or would you choose someone who has to learn his job through trial and error?

☐ HER REPLY ☐ HIS REPLY

☐ HIS REPLY ☐ HER REPLY

What's going on in your head now?

☐ HER REPLY ☐ HIS REPLY

☐ HIS REPLY ☐ HER REPLY

Would you rather do the whole thing over again?

☐ HER REPLY ☐ HIS REPLY   ☐ HIS REPLY ☐ HER REPLY

Would you rather be rich than dead?

☐ HER REPLY ☐ HIS REPLY   ☐ HIS REPLY ☐ HER REPLY

What is one thing that you've learned that has changed your entire mindset?

☐ HER REPLY ☐ HIS REPLY   ☐ HIS REPLY ☐ HER REPLY

Where do you live your everyday life?

☐ HER REPLY ☐ HIS REPLY   ☐ HIS REPLY ☐ HER REPLY

What were the odds of that happening?

☐ HER REPLY   ☐ HIS REPLY   ☐ HIS REPLY   ☐ HER REPLY

How would you describe your house to someone who has never visited there before?

☐ HER REPLY   ☐ HIS REPLY   ☐ HIS REPLY   ☐ HER REPLY

What do you like to wear?

☐ HER REPLY ☐ HIS REPLY   ☐ HIS REPLY ☐ HER REPLY

What do you need to know now?

☐ HER REPLY ☐ HIS REPLY   ☐ HIS REPLY ☐ HER REPLY

If you could have a superpower, what would it be?

☐ HER REPLY ☐ HIS REPLY

☐ HIS REPLY ☐ HER REPLY

What would you do if someone did something wrong?

☐ HER REPLY ☐ HIS REPLY

☐ HIS REPLY ☐ HER REPLY

What is one thing you could not live without?

☐ HER REPLY   ☐ HIS REPLY

☐ HIS REPLY   ☐ HER REPLY

What's your favorite type of pizza crust?

☐ HER REPLY   ☐ HIS REPLY

☐ HIS REPLY   ☐ HER REPLY

Why do you think he./she does that?

☐ HER REPLY   ☐ HIS REPLY   ☐ HIS REPLY   ☐ HER REPLY

Why do you get so worked up over this?

☐ HER REPLY   ☐ HIS REPLY   ☐ HIS REPLY   ☐ HER REPLY

How many times have you been stuck?

☐ HER REPLY ☐ HIS REPLY   ☐ HIS REPLY ☐ HER REPLY

What is one thing that you've done that has made you better?

☐ HER REPLY ☐ HIS REPLY   ☐ HIS REPLY ☐ HER REPLY

List of things that you haven't done yet but were checked by someone else

☐ HER REPLY ☐ HIS REPLY   ☐ HIS REPLY ☐ HER REPLY

Why do you think you can make the world a more meaningful place?

☐ HER REPLY ☐ HIS REPLY   ☐ HIS REPLY ☐ HER REPLY

What is it like being at your happiest at the worst time?

☐ HER REPLY ☐ HIS REPLY   ☐ HIS REPLY ☐ HER REPLY

If you could do something just like your friend (use the name of friend), what would you do?

☐ HER REPLY ☐ HIS REPLY   ☐ HIS REPLY ☐ HER REPLY

What is the most significant battle in your head?

☐ HER REPLY ☐ HIS REPLY

☐ HIS REPLY ☐ HER REPLY

What are some tips and tricks to use when organizing your day and your life to optimize your day to day life?

☐ HER REPLY ☐ HIS REPLY

☐ HIS REPLY ☐ HER REPLY

If you could change one thing in your life, what would it be?

☐ HER REPLY ☐ HIS REPLY   ☐ HIS REPLY ☐ HER REPLY

How would you describe the feeling of being afraid of the unknown?

☐ HER REPLY ☐ HIS REPLY   ☐ HIS REPLY ☐ HER REPLY

What fictional place would you most like to go?

☐ HER REPLY ☐ HIS REPLY   ☐ HIS REPLY ☐ HER REPLY

20 Reasons why you love your favorite TV show.

☐ HER REPLY ☐ HIS REPLY   ☐ HIS REPLY ☐ HER REPLY

What is the most significant customer experience you've ever had?

☐ HER REPLY ☐ HIS REPLY

☐ HIS REPLY ☐ HER REPLY

What is the one thing that goes in it that others will not?

☐ HER REPLY ☐ HIS REPLY

☐ HIS REPLY ☐ HER REPLY

If you had to choose one city to live in for the next 20 years, which would you choose?

☐ HER REPLY ☐ HIS REPLY

☐ HIS REPLY ☐ HER REPLY

What is the worst quote you've ever heard?

☐ HER REPLY ☐ HIS REPLY

☐ HIS REPLY ☐ HER REPLY

Would you rather be married to yourself? Why?

☐ HER REPLY ☐ HIS REPLY   ☐ HIS REPLY ☐ HER REPLY

How would you describe the feeling of being connected with life?

☐ HER REPLY ☐ HIS REPLY   ☐ HIS REPLY ☐ HER REPLY

How can you improve your happiness?

☐ HER REPLY ☐ HIS REPLY

☐ HIS REPLY ☐ HER REPLY

If you had to choose just one thing to be given, what would it be?

☐ HER REPLY ☐ HIS REPLY

☐ HIS REPLY ☐ HER REPLY

What would you put in a time capsule to be opened by the next generation?

☐ HER REPLY ☐ HIS REPLY

☐ HIS REPLY ☐ HER REPLY

How do you talk to your children and pets?

☐ HER REPLY ☐ HIS REPLY

☐ HIS REPLY ☐ HER REPLY

If you could be one thing for the rest of your life, what would it be and why?

☐ HER REPLY ☐ HIS REPLY   ☐ HIS REPLY ☐ HER REPLY

What was it you wanted to say?

☐ HER REPLY ☐ HIS REPLY   ☐ HIS REPLY ☐ HER REPLY

If you could change anything about the past world, what would it be?

☐ HER REPLY ☐ HIS REPLY

☐ HIS REPLY ☐ HER REPLY

List of things that you can't judge one way or the other

☐ HER REPLY ☐ HIS REPLY

☐ HIS REPLY ☐ HER REPLY

List of things that you need to worry about

☐ HER REPLY   ☐ HIS REPLY   ☐ HIS REPLY   ☐ HER REPLY

What's your greatest accomplishment?

☐ HER REPLY   ☐ HIS REPLY   ☐ HIS REPLY   ☐ HER REPLY

Do you have a fear of losing your job? Why?

☐ HER REPLY ☐ HIS REPLY   ☐ HIS REPLY ☐ HER REPLY

What is the most significant thing you've ever learned?

☐ HER REPLY ☐ HIS REPLY   ☐ HIS REPLY ☐ HER REPLY

What's the benefit for you knowing someone else's point of view?

☐ HER REPLY   ☐ HIS REPLY   ☐ HIS REPLY   ☐ HER REPLY

Do you think the world has gone crazy?

☐ HER REPLY   ☐ HIS REPLY   ☐ HIS REPLY   ☐ HER REPLY

How do you feel on a warm sunny day?

☐ HER REPLY ☐ HIS REPLY

☐ HIS REPLY ☐ HER REPLY

Why do you think you are the way you are?

☐ HER REPLY ☐ HIS REPLY

☐ HIS REPLY ☐ HER REPLY

What is the one thing that kept you from selling out?

☐ HER REPLY ☐ HIS REPLY   ☐ HIS REPLY ☐ HER REPLY

If you could be the one person to tell the story of how you started on the right path in life, what would that be?

☐ HER REPLY ☐ HIS REPLY   ☐ HIS REPLY ☐ HER REPLY

What kind of parent do you think you will be?

☐ HER REPLY ☐ HIS REPLY

☐ HIS REPLY ☐ HER REPLY

If you had to spend your whole life working for one person, what would you do? Why?

☐ HER REPLY ☐ HIS REPLY

☐ HIS REPLY ☐ HER REPLY

What has the experience been like working for other people?

☐ HER REPLY ☐ HIS REPLY   ☐ HIS REPLY ☐ HER REPLY

Describe a major environmental problem and what you believe should be done about it.

☐ HER REPLY ☐ HIS REPLY   ☐ HIS REPLY ☐ HER REPLY

What is one thing that makes you want to change something about yourself?

☐ HER REPLY ☐ HIS REPLY

☐ HIS REPLY ☐ HER REPLY

What is the one book you would still want to give to people who have never read it?

☐ HER REPLY ☐ HIS REPLY

☐ HIS REPLY ☐ HER REPLY

How would you describe the feeling of being so emotionally balanced?

☐ HER REPLY ☐ HIS REPLY   ☐ HIS REPLY ☐ HER REPLY

How do you deal with this lack of control?

☐ HER REPLY ☐ HIS REPLY   ☐ HIS REPLY ☐ HER REPLY

What would you say to those that are trying to tell you that you can't become an important person?

☐ HER REPLY ☐ HIS REPLY

☐ HIS REPLY ☐ HER REPLY

What's your plan to get there?

☐ HER REPLY ☐ HIS REPLY

☐ HIS REPLY ☐ HER REPLY

What is your favorite food and why?

☐ HER REPLY ☐ HIS REPLY ☐ HIS REPLY ☐ HER REPLY

List of things that could cause an error either trivial or serious

☐ HER REPLY ☐ HIS REPLY ☐ HIS REPLY ☐ HER REPLY

Who is your favorite storybook character?

☐ HER REPLY ☐ HIS REPLY

☐ HIS REPLY ☐ HER REPLY

What can you do to have your voice heard?

☐ HER REPLY ☐ HIS REPLY

☐ HIS REPLY ☐ HER REPLY

What is the one thing that most defines how your body experiences and looks in your youth?

☐ HER REPLY ☐ HIS REPLY   ☐ HIS REPLY ☐ HER REPLY

If you could be more than the sum of your experiences, what would it be?

☐ HER REPLY ☐ HIS REPLY   ☐ HIS REPLY ☐ HER REPLY

What do you think or believe in yourself today?

☐ HER REPLY ☐ HIS REPLY   ☐ HIS REPLY ☐ HER REPLY

What do you prefer? Being drunk or sober? Why?

☐ HER REPLY ☐ HIS REPLY   ☐ HIS REPLY ☐ HER REPLY

Who do you see dealing with the most problems?

☐ HER REPLY ☐ HIS REPLY   ☐ HIS REPLY ☐ HER REPLY

What is it about you that is the most difficult?

☐ HER REPLY ☐ HIS REPLY   ☐ HIS REPLY ☐ HER REPLY

What would the day be like if everyone could change their personalities?

☐ HER REPLY ☐ HIS REPLY

☐ HIS REPLY ☐ HER REPLY

If you had to choose one thing that is your biggest achievement, what would it be?

☐ HER REPLY ☐ HIS REPLY

☐ HIS REPLY ☐ HER REPLY

What do you dislike about yourself?

☐ HER REPLY ☐ HIS REPLY

☐ HIS REPLY ☐ HER REPLY

List of things you liked

☐ HER REPLY ☐ HIS REPLY

☐ HIS REPLY ☐ HER REPLY

What question would you most like to know the answer to?

☐ HER REPLY ☐ HIS REPLY

☐ HIS REPLY ☐ HER REPLY

How would you describe the feeling of being drunk?

☐ HER REPLY ☐ HIS REPLY

☐ HIS REPLY ☐ HER REPLY

Do you turn into a robot when you experience failure? Why?

☐ HER REPLY ☐ HIS REPLY   ☐ HIS REPLY ☐ HER REPLY

Describe the chores and responsibilities that you have at home.

☐ HER REPLY ☐ HIS REPLY   ☐ HIS REPLY ☐ HER REPLY

What's the most challenging part of playing live?

☐ HER REPLY ☐ HIS REPLY

☐ HIS REPLY ☐ HER REPLY

How do you feel about the things that you do?

☐ HER REPLY ☐ HIS REPLY

☐ HIS REPLY ☐ HER REPLY

If you could choose, which era would you have liked to have been born into and why?

☐ HER REPLY ☐ HIS REPLY   ☐ HIS REPLY ☐ HER REPLY

What do your daughters look for in a lover?

☐ HER REPLY ☐ HIS REPLY   ☐ HIS REPLY ☐ HER REPLY

If you could have one job you would do for free, what would it be?

☐ HER REPLY ☐ HIS REPLY

☐ HIS REPLY ☐ HER REPLY

What was the last picture you bought?

☐ HER REPLY ☐ HIS REPLY

☐ HIS REPLY ☐ HER REPLY

If you could be another person for five minutes, who would it be and why?

☐ HER REPLY ☐ HIS REPLY   ☐ HIS REPLY ☐ HER REPLY

Do you believe in aliens, faeries, or mermaids? Why? Why not?

☐ HER REPLY ☐ HIS REPLY   ☐ HIS REPLY ☐ HER REPLY

If you could look back at your life, what would you want to know about yourself?

☐ HER REPLY   ☐ HIS REPLY

☐ HIS REPLY   ☐ HER REPLY

What would it take to make you change your mind?

☐ HER REPLY   ☐ HIS REPLY

☐ HIS REPLY   ☐ HER REPLY

If you could have lunch with three people, who would you
have lunch with?

☐ HER REPLY ☐ HIS REPLY   ☐ HIS REPLY ☐ HER REPLY

If you were to start your own company, what would it be?

☐ HER REPLY ☐ HIS REPLY   ☐ HIS REPLY ☐ HER REPLY

How do you deal with the reality of the way you're used to living?

☐ HER REPLY ☐ HIS REPLY

☐ HIS REPLY ☐ HER REPLY

What do you want for your birthday?

☐ HER REPLY ☐ HIS REPLY

☐ HIS REPLY ☐ HER REPLY

What kind of fun projects do you like to work on?

☐ HER REPLY ☐ HIS REPLY

☐ HIS REPLY ☐ HER REPLY

List of things that have made family and relationships more difficult over time

☐ HER REPLY ☐ HIS REPLY

☐ HIS REPLY ☐ HER REPLY

Would you rather make your own dinner or buy a gift?

☐ HER REPLY ☐ HIS REPLY   ☐ HIS REPLY ☐ HER REPLY

If you could only go back two years, how do you think you would have done differently?

☐ HER REPLY ☐ HIS REPLY   ☐ HIS REPLY ☐ HER REPLY

Where do you think you will be in five years?

☐ HER REPLY ☐ HIS REPLY   ☐ HIS REPLY ☐ HER REPLY

If you could take out all the things you can't manage, everything you hate about yourself, every thought that makes you uncomfortable, what's it going to be like to go back and live with the past?

☐ HER REPLY ☐ HIS REPLY   ☐ HIS REPLY ☐ HER REPLY

What if God would not judge us but you could, how would
you go about it?

☐ HER REPLY ☐ HIS REPLY   ☐ HIS REPLY ☐ HER REPLY

If you could pick one piece of clothing, what would it be and
why?

☐ HER REPLY ☐ HIS REPLY   ☐ HIS REPLY ☐ HER REPLY

What does your child want in a boyfriend/girlfriend?

☐ HER REPLY ☐ HIS REPLY   ☐ HIS REPLY ☐ HER REPLY

What can you do to make that happen?

☐ HER REPLY ☐ HIS REPLY   ☐ HIS REPLY ☐ HER REPLY

How do you respond to your critics?

☐ HER REPLY ☐ HIS REPLY   ☐ HIS REPLY ☐ HER REPLY

What is one thing that you miss?

☐ HER REPLY ☐ HIS REPLY   ☐ HIS REPLY ☐ HER REPLY

Think of your favorite toy. Why do you like it best?

☐ HER REPLY ☐ HIS REPLY

☐ HIS REPLY ☐ HER REPLY

List of things that go away with sleep

☐ HER REPLY ☐ HIS REPLY

☐ HIS REPLY ☐ HER REPLY

If you had to choose one thing you are doing differently this year, what would it be?

☐ HER REPLY ☐ HIS REPLY   ☐ HIS REPLY ☐ HER REPLY

What's the saddest movie you've ever seen?

☐ HER REPLY ☐ HIS REPLY   ☐ HIS REPLY ☐ HER REPLY

What is one thing that you can be sure of?

☐ HER REPLY ☐ HIS REPLY

☐ HIS REPLY ☐ HER REPLY

If you had to choose one thing you'd love to change about how you look for the rest of your life, what would it be?

☐ HER REPLY ☐ HIS REPLY

☐ HIS REPLY ☐ HER REPLY

What does "there are two sides to every coin" mean to you?

☐ HER REPLY ☐ HIS REPLY   ☐ HIS REPLY ☐ HER REPLY

If you could have anything you wanted, what would it be?

☐ HER REPLY ☐ HIS REPLY   ☐ HIS REPLY ☐ HER REPLY

How would you describe the feeling of being naked in front
of a big crowd and then just disappearing?

☐ HER REPLY ☐ HIS REPLY   ☐ HIS REPLY ☐ HER REPLY

Why do you think you've got your name?

☐ HER REPLY ☐ HIS REPLY   ☐ HIS REPLY ☐ HER REPLY